The Divine Armour of God

Spiritual Weaponry for Daily Warfare

RAMSEY WATCHMAN

DEDICATION

Dedicated to Akvile

CONTENTS

FOREWORD

When I was very young I remember kneeling tentatively at the top of the stairs, together with my brothers and my mother before a little altar to the Lord Jesus and the Virgin Mary. Night after night we would recite a decade of the Rosary, 10 Hail Marys and an Our Father, my brothers and I trying desperately not to laugh for fear of the wrath of the wooden spoon!

Until recently this precious memory lay dormant in me, hidden like a long-lost treasure. What an example this mother showed her children. What a deep sense of faith she instilled. And what spiritual training. I would like to thank her for it.

Today I am slowly, but as evidenced by this very book, surely realising the power of God to move mountains.

Never stop believing, never give up and never give in, especially in the darkest hour. Trust God to move your mountain. The victory is already yours in Jesus Christ.

ACKNOWLEDGMENTS

I would like to thank my parents for all their support and
my family. I would also like to acknowledge all the
Christian believers who are working tirelessly and boldly to
spread the Gospel and the many pastors who have
influenced and educated my faith.
And I would like to thank David Malocco
for his help in design and formatting.

AMDG

SYNOPSIS

The Divine Armour of God is a manuscript based on a specific passage of Scripture from The Bible, found in St. Paul's letter to the Ephesians, chapter 6, verses 13-17.

This text outlines the spiritual or Divine Armour made available to us as Christians, through our belief in Jesus' death and resurrection, and our faith. Like any armour, the purpose of this Divine Armour is protection in battle. *The Divine Armour of God* makes the analogy of the battle of our daily lives and shines a light on God's gift of spiritual protection which takes the form of specific pieces of spiritual armour. The armour is a supernatural shield against negative influences and attacks, resulting in a divinely healthy, joyful and prosperous life.

The purpose of *The Divine Armour of God* is to inform

people of invaluable information contained in the Bible which does not seem to be widely known, even amongst Christians. This "information" is divinely ordained and the intent of writing this manuscript is to open up a new world for people that will be a revelation.

The world is experiencing arguably unprecedented social, geopolitical and natural upheaval and *The Divine Armour of God* is intended as a daily manual of protection, inspiration and hope for times such as these. A sort of training manual, that when it is read, will qualify another Divine Soldier of God!

2018 was the 70th Anniversary of the founding of Israel as a nation, an important factor in considering the appeal of a manuscript such as this. And America, under President Trump made the historic decision to move the US Embassy from Tel Aviv to Jerusalem, coinciding with this 70th Anniversary and highlighting the land of Israel and the Jewish people, the land and the people around which The Bible is based.

I believe for believers this manuscript is timely and necessary. For non-believers it could be the book that changes their lives.

Ephesians 6: 13-17 likens the Divine Armour of God to the armour of the Roman soldiers of the day, occupiers of the Holy Land at that time. The full armour of God comprises the Belt of Truth, the

Breastplate of Righteousness, the Shoes of Peace, the Helmet of Salvation, the Shield of Faith and the Sword of the Spirit.

The Divine Armour of God comprises an opening, an introduction and 8 subsequent chapters.

The opening acquaints us with part of Scripture found in Ephesians chapter 6, verses 10-12, a precursor to the main scriptural passage on which the narrative of the manuscript is based.

The introduction, provides the background setting for the "gift" of the armour, namely God's un-quantifiably deep love for us and His ultimate sacrifice, His Son Jesus Christ on the Cross, for the salvation of the whole world.

The main body of the manuscript contains 7 chapters. Chapter 1 introduces us to the armour, piece by piece, and sets up the potential power of the armour when it is "worn". The next 6 chapters are dedicated, one each, to the 6 pieces of armour.

Each chapter details the characteristics of each piece of armour, its supernatural qualities and its relevance to the real world and for daily living. The message is that "wearing" this spiritual armour will equip the reader with everything they need for total victory in the battle of their daily lives.

The final chapter, chapter 8, entitled "The Divine

Soldier", is a thought-provoking, empowering and uplifting climax, equipping the reader with information that could transform their lives.

The message of the concluding chapter is for the reader to "put on" the Divine Armour and go out into the world as a "Soldier of God", living under divine protection, with courage, assuredness, purpose, hope, joy and a spirit of total victory!

OPENING

EPHESIANS 6: 10: "Finally, my brethren, be strong in the Lord, and in the power of his might.

EPHESIANS 6: 11: "Put on the whole armour of God, that ye may be able to stand against the wiles of the devil.

EPHESIANS 6: 12: "For we wrestle not against flesh and blood, but against principalities, against powers, against the rulers of the darkness of this world, against spiritual wickedness in high *places*."

"El Shaddai, El Shaddai…"…

…a desperate cry hearkened, piercing the cold air like an arrow shot straight toward the sun…..

… *"El Shaddai"*…

INTRODUCTION

God the Father is the all-powerful, all-knowing and almighty Creator of the heavens and the earth and of all things. He is also a divinely loving father and a loving God. So strong and powerful is His love for us that he gave up His only begotten Son to be sacrificed as a sin offering for the salvation of the whole world.

JOHN 3: 16: "For God so loved the world, that he gave his only begotten Son, that whosoever believeth in him should not perish, but have everlasting life."

Jesus Christ became our sin, so that we might become His righteousness. He died so that we might have everlasting life. He bore our sicknesses so that we might enjoy divine health. He took our judgement so that we might be spared the judgement of sinners. A divine transaction, He paid the ultimate fine for our divine freedom…freedom from sin, sickness and disease, poverty, fear and death.

A free gift of amazing Grace, unmerited favour, through the blood of the Lord Jesus on the Cross, given to us by a Father whose love as demonstrated, surpasses all understanding.

ISAIAH 53:4: "Surely he hath borne our griefs, and carried our sorrows: yet we did esteem him stricken, smitten of God, and afflicted."

ISAIAH 53:5: "But he *was* wounded for our transgressions, *he was* bruised for our iniquities: the chastisement of our peace *was* upon him; and with his stripes we are healed."

The gift and the Gospel of Grace freely given to all, but only truly received by all those born again by baptism in the Holy Spirit through Jesus Christ.

In conversation with a Pharisee named Nicodemus, Jesus said;

JOHN 3:3: "...Verily, verily, I say unto thee, Except a man be born again, he cannot see the kingdom of God."

JOHN 3:4: "Nicodemus saith unto him, How can a man be born when he is old? can he enter the second time into his mother's womb, and be born?"

JOHN 3:5: "Jesus answered, Verily, verily, I say unto thee, Except a man be born of water and *of* the Spirit, he cannot enter into the kingdom of God."

JOHN 3:6: "That which is born of the flesh is flesh; and that which is born of the Spirit is spirit."

As any loving father provides for his children, so it is with our Heavenly Father to a degree that is difficult for us to understand.

MATTHEW 7:11: "If ye then, being evil, know how to give good gifts unto your children, how much more shall your Father which is in heaven give good things to them that ask him?"

MATTHEW 7:7: "Ask, and it shall be given you; seek, and ye shall find; knock, and it shall be opened unto you:"

MATTHEW 7: 8: "For every one that asketh receiveth; and he that seeketh findeth; and to him that knocketh it shall be opened."

…and so it is that our Father in Heaven has provided for all His children a personal armour and weaponry of such power that it will forever keep all who receive and believe, all who wear and wield it, steadfast, strong, safe, secure, joyful, prosperous, at peace and victorious. Through the Divine Armour of God, victory is guaranteed in the battlefield of our daily lives, from attacks in our physical world and beyond.

1 INTRODUCTION TO THE ARMOUR

EPHESIANS 6: 13: "Wherefore take unto you the whole armour of God, that ye may be able to withstand in the evil day, and having done all, to stand."

EPHESIANS 6: 14: "Stand therefore, having your loins girt about with truth, and having on the breastplate of righteousness;"

EPHESIANS 6: 15: "And your feet shod with the preparation of the gospel of peace;"

EPHESIANS 6: 16: "Above all, taking the shield of faith, wherewith ye shall be able to quench all the fiery darts of the wicked."

EPHESIANS 6: 17: "And take the helmet of salvation, and the sword of the Spirit, which is the word of God:"

Monday, Monday. Another week. That familiar feeling. The alarm clock sounds like it is impatient and two hours premature. Instead of wanting to retreat back under the covers, imagine you wake thankful for the gift of a new day, for the gift of your health, air in your lungs, a healthy body, family, friends, nature and animals, your God-given talents, your hobbies which you love to do, and so much more…

… imagine then knowing that you have received the ultimate gift…divine provision and protection from your Heavenly Father so that you can go freely about your day absolutely safe and secure, full of joy and peace, with a supernatural protection over your body, mind, soul, spirit and your life.

It is written in 3rd JOHN 2: "Beloved, I wish above all things that thou mayest prosper and be in health, even as thy soul prospereth."

There is a belief and a lot of confusion amongst many Christians and amongst the Church that we serve a perennially angry God, an impatient God, a demanding God. However, in essence, these doctrines are outdated. They go back 2,000 years.

For all, He is a God of unquantifiable love and longsuffering patience. However, this love and patience has a limit for those who reject Jesus and turn their backs on God and that limit will be made manifest in the final Judgement written about in the book of Revelation. Before that time comes, which the Bible states "of that day and hour knoweth no man", those who continue to reject Jesus and reject God without truly repenting before they pass, will receive the Judgement of sinners.

Yes, living as a true Christian is demanding, but God through the Grace that comes by the death and resurrection of His beloved Son Jesus Christ, *is* the God of unquantifiable, unending love and patience. He is also the God of provision, prosperity and supernatural supply.

With the life, death and resurrection of our Lord Jesus Christ, the Law, or full adherence to the Ten Commandments for salvation was replaced by Grace. And where the Law demanded good works and perfect obedience to its ordinances for salvation, Grace brings forth a never-ending supply of forgiveness of all sins past, present and future, of peace, of provision, of protection and of the righteousness of God through faith.

1st CORINTHIANS 15: 55-57 provides a clear distinction between the demands and consequences of the Law and the game-changing gift of Grace through our Lord Jesus Christ.

1st CORINTHIANS 15: 55:   "O death, where *is* thy sting? O grave, where *is* thy victory?"

1st CORINTHIANS 15: 56:   "The sting of death *is* sin; and the strength of sin *is* the law."

1st CORINTHIANS 15: 57:   "But thanks *be* to God, which giveth us the victory through our Lord Jesus Christ."

Through the gift of Grace, the unmerited favour of God, all our needs are met forever and all of our sins are forgiven past, present and future.

It is written in COLOSSIANS 2: 13-14, "And you, being dead in your sins and the uncircumcision of your flesh, hath he quickened together with him, having forgiven you all trespasses;"

"Blotting out the handwriting of ordinances that was against us, which was contrary to us, and took it out of the way, nailing it to his cross;"

Clearly here it is written that all our trespasses are forgiven and the handwriting of ordinances that was against us, or the Law by the Ten Commandments, has been blotted out and nailed to the cross. Jesus, the only innocent man who ever lived, the only pure man to ever walk the earth, the only man who ever lived who knew no sin, was nailed to the cross where he became our sin so that we might become His righteousness through the Grace of God and through faith.

2nd CORINTHIANS 5: 21: "For he hath made him *to be* sin for us, who knew no sin; that we might be made the righteousness of God in him."

So, as believers, we are clearly under God's everlasting Grace, forever under His unmerited and undeserved favour. God has made available to us the provision, the protection and supply of everything we can ever need to live a life of joy, peace of mind, body, soul and spirit and total victory, against any adversity EVERY DAY of our lives....the sacred key to the chest of armour....only to believe and to receive.

ROMANS 8: 37: "Nay, in all these things we are more than conquerors through him that loved us."

Scripture clearly states in EPHESIANS 6: 12: "For we wrestle not against flesh and blood, but against principalities, against powers, against the rulers of the darkness of this world, against spiritual wickedness in high *places*."

It is also written that "My people are destroyed for lack of knowledge..." – HOSEA 4: 6

...How many Christians today know of the spiritual battle we are in the midst of, and the weaponry that is available to us in combat, in our daily lives?

Scripture also tells us that "...the wages of sin *is*

death; but the gift of God *is* eternal life through Jesus Christ our Lord." – ROMANS 6: 23

While "death" here does not necessarily mean a physical death, it can mean the death of a relationship, a marriage, some aspect of your health, your finances or part or all of your faith. So God has lovingly and graciously provided us His Divine Armour to protect us from temptation and sin and from every attack on our body, our mind, on our spirit, our soul and on our lives.

3rd JOHN 2: "Beloved, I wish above all things that thou mayest prosper and be in health, even as thy soul prospereth."

God has made available to us a divine armour and arsenal so powerful it will triumph over every adversary, of flesh and blood or supernatural!

EPHESIANS 6: 11: "Put on the whole armour of God, that ye may be able to stand against the wiles of the devil."

2nd CORINTHIANS 5: 17: "Therefore if any man *be* in Christ, *he is* a new creature: old things are passed away; behold, all things are become new."

Have you accepted Jesus Christ as your personal saviour and Lord over your life? If not, do so TODAY.

ROMANS 10: 13: "For whosoever shall call upon the name of the Lord shall be saved."

PSALMS 91: 15: "He shall call upon me, and I will answer him: I *will be* with him in trouble; I will deliver him, and honour him."

For those already in Jesus...step out boldly as that "new creature"...step into and take up your divine armour and weaponry...

...stand tall, upright and strong and gird yourself with the Belt of Truth, strap on the Breastplate of Righteousness, put on the Helmet of Salvation, step into the Shoes of Peace, raise the Shield of Faith and wield the Sword of the Spirit...

...congratulations...you are a new creation in Christ...a divinely powerful soldier in the army of the Lord!

2 THE BELT OF TRUTH

EPHESIANS 6: 14:   "Stand therefore, having your loins girt about with truth…"

"Do you solemnly swear that you will tell the truth the whole truth and nothing but the truth so help you God?"

With a hand placed on the Holy Bible, this scenario plays out every day in courts of law around the world. The truth is inextricably and legally linked with the Word of God.

Written by the Apostle Paul, the Epistle or letter to the Ephesians likens the Divine Armour and Weaponry of God to the armour and weaponry worn and carried by the Roman soldiers of the day, occupiers of the Holy Land at that time. This armour was designed to protect the most vital parts and organs of the body from any attack. And so the analogy is made with the spiritual Weaponry and Armour of God: The first piece of armour Paul mentions is the Belt of Truth.

The belt worn by a Roman soldier was a strong and sturdy leather strapping which held the soldier's most important offensive weapon his sword. So the analogy connects truth with the Word of God, the sword being the "Spirit of God" or His Word.

Jesus said "…I am the way, the truth, and the life: no man cometh unto the Father, but by me" – JOHN 14: 6.

The importance of truth in daily living and in our lives is expressly apparent since Jesus Himself is the truth and the truth is part of our divine armour.

The truth all too often gets mixed up in opinion. And when a view or opinion is expressed and reinforced through repetition over time, it can become a person's truth, despite not being the actual truth. When it comes to the truth, there are no opinions, there is no debate, there is only fact. For the truth is fact. Nothing more and nothing less.

The truth carries a certain sound, it has a certain ring to it. It puts out a certain vibrational wave. It is a frequency of fact picked up by our intuitive antenna and it always rings true. The truth is a peaceful sound and it is simple and without blemish. The very same attributes as the embodiment of truth, the risen Christ Jesus. And like Him, the truth is incorruptible.

When the truth is spoken, it is heard and it is known. It is without distortion or confusion. The truth always stands alone, unshakeable and untouchable. The truth is the truth precisely because it can stand alone. The enemy of the truth is the lie and deceit. One cannot exist without the other. The truth can stand on its own but a lie cannot exist without the truth simply because it is not fact and it is not truth. It is a shadowy and shady reflection of itself. A nothingness that has no substance. And this is where the truth's essence of purity shines a blinding light upon its dark and murky antithesis.

Like the truth, the lie too has its own sound, in extreme contrast to the pure resonance of truth. It is a loud, unsubtle, chaotic cacophony of distorted energetic confusion that is at odds with the harmonious harmonics of everything around it. It can be heard and picked up, a mile away.

We always have to be truth seekers, and consciously aware and vigilant of attacks on truth. Deception is a master-weapon of the enemy. Deception, distortion, chaos and inversion. He will try to make anything natural, unnatural and anything unnatural, natural. He will try to make anything normal, abnormal and anything abnormal, normal. (Normal here means anything that is normal truth). He seeks to twist and taint anything that is pure, to make it impure. He will attack, accuse and try to pervert the truth with deception. And this enemy takes no days off and has no need for rest.

GALATIANS 1: 7: "...there be some that trouble you, and would pervert the gospel of Christ."

Standing tall and upright in full conviction wearing the Belt of Truth, we have to be ever watchful, alert and aware of his attacks on truth. The truth is always simple, because it is fact. The lie is a complicated mess. The idiom "the devil is in the detail" rings true.

REVELATION 12: 9: "And the great dragon was cast out, that old serpent, called the Devil, and Satan, which deceiveth the whole world..."

The Bible speaks of the importance of being aware of deception in the "Last Days" or the "End Times":

MATTHEW 24: 24: "For there shall arise false Christs, and false prophets, and shall shew great signs and wonders; insomuch that, if *it were* possible, they shall deceive the very elect."

The "elect" here being the "body of Christ" or the Church.

MATTHEW 24: 4: "And Jesus answered and said unto them, Take heed that no man deceive you."

MATTHEW 24: 5: "For many shall come in my name, saying, I am Christ; and shall deceive many."

JESUS CHRIST *IS* TRUTH, and when we are in Him, we operate, we live in truth.

There is no peace in the lie.

MARK 8: 36: "For what shall it profit a man, if he shall gain the whole world, and lose his own soul?"

Only by hearing, speaking, living the truth can we be fully protected from direct and indirect attacks by "the deceiver of the whole world" and by those slaves to his false doctrine.

In the age we live in, the importance of truth has never been greater. We live in a time when a threatening phenomenon which has become known as "fake news" has invaded the social and political landscape bringing confusion and distortion into our daily lives. It is getting more and more difficult to verify the authenticity of news stories and in many instances to know which narrative to believe.

However JESUS CHRIST *IS* TRUTH. As believers in Him, we can use our God-given intuition and wisdom to help discern the truth from the lie. His Gospel is the Gospel of Good News. Forget fake news. Keep your ears and your heart attuned to the Good News.

1st KINGS 4: 29 does indeed prove that God imparts

wisdom, understanding and intuition to those loyal and faithful of His flock: "And God gave Solomon wisdom and understanding exceeding much, and largeness of heart, even as the sand that *is* on the sea shore."

…and that's a lot of sand!

When in doubt, don't ask yourself what you think about the situation. This will provide you with an ego-based, bias and societally-skewed "answer", a learned response. Rather ask yourself "how does this feel to me?", "how do I feel about it?", "how does this sound?"

Your subconscious, your intuition, your inner-voice and God-given wisdom will never lead you far from the truth. Even when the whole world is clamouring their approval to the contrary.

JESUS CHRIST *IS* TRUTH. In Him is available to us "exceeding much" wisdom and understanding. Believe it, receive it and utilise it EVERY DAY, to discern truth in all situations, for the betterment of your life, your loved ones and the world.

Let truth be your anchor, just as the belt holds the garments of battle together. Be anchored in the Lord Jesus and you will be safe and secure in truth in your daily life, even in the most tumultuous season of your life.

Know the truth. Hear it. Speak it. Live in it EVERY DAY. For Jesus is the way, the truth and the life, and the truth shall set you free.

3 THE BRESTPLATE OF RIGHTEOUSNESS

EPHESIANS 6: 14: "Stand therefore, having your loins girt about with truth, and having on the breastplate of righteousness;"

Standing tall, strong and secure in the Belt of Truth, next it is time to strap on the centre-piece of your amour and protection, the Breastplate of Righteousness.

In the times of the Roman Empire, the breastplate was of crucial importance, protecting the vital organs of the soldier's body, such as the lungs, from attack, and the most critical organ of all the heart. Without the breastplate it would mean certain death for the soldier, the torso and heart open, exposed and completely vulnerable. A robust breastplate provided the necessary protection for the entire torso and the heart. The attacks would still come but they would not penetrate the armour. A soldier could confidently navigate the battlefield with conviction, his most vital organ fully shielded and protected.

For the foot-soldier of God, the Breastplate of Righteousness is too the centre-point and centre-piece of this warrior's armour and protection. Without it he leaves his most vital organ, his heart, exposed and vulnerable to all manner of attack by the enemy.

MATTHEW 5: 8: "Blessed *are* the pure in heart: for they shall see God."

Jesus Christ gave Himself up on the cross to be crucified for every one of us. By becoming our sin and taking our punishment and our judgement, believers become the righteousness of God in Him. This is in itself the very heart of the Bible and the very heart of the covenant of Grace. Through the blood of Jesus, everlasting life is made available to every one of us by Grace through faith. And by this unmerited and undeserved favour, those who believe become the righteousness of God Himself!

And when we repent of our sins and receive Jesus as Lord and Saviour, God never sees us as sin, He only ever sees us as His righteousness....otherwise the death of His beloved Son would be in vain!

This is the beauty, the gift, the miracle that is righteousness through Grace and the Cross.

ROMANS 5: 19: "For as by one man's disobedience many were made sinners, so by the obedience of one shall many be made righteous."

ROMANS 5: 20: "Moreover the law entered, that the offence might abound. But where sin abounded, grace did much more abound:"

ROMANS 5: 21: "That as sin hath reigned unto death, even so might grace reign through righteousness unto eternal life by Jesus Christ our Lord."

Here we see the stark reality that the Law equals sin and death and Grace through righteousness equals everlasting life in Jesus Christ. This is not to say that the Law or the Ten Commandments are made redundant. It remains God's Holy Law and perfect in itself. But as born sinners, imperfect in a fallen world, it has always been impossible and unattainable, the keeping of the Ten Commandments.

"The Law entered that the offence might abound." Indeed in JAMES 2:10 we see that the breaking of one Commandment means being guilty of breaking all: "For whosoever shall keep the whole law, and yet offend in one *point*, he is guilty of all."

So the gift of Grace was given through the blood of Jesus that we might be saved from the yoke of salvation through "good works", and that we would receive everlasting life by believing in Jesus' death and resurrection and accepting Him as Lord and Saviour.

There is a lot of discussion about Grace being a license to go out and sin, but on the contrary, Grace empowers us to be more holy and to want to walk, talk and live in righteousness. What a wonderful gift we have received. Truly Amazing Grace!

It is written in 1st JOHN 4: 17: "Herein is our love made perfect, that we may have boldness in the day of judgement: because as he is, so are we in this world."

This incredible verse highlights the magnitude of what has been made available to us through the death and resurrection of Jesus. "As he is, so are we in this world." Notice it says as he "*is*", not as he "was" but as he "*IS*"......as the Lord Jesus *is* at the Father's right hand, so are we in this world!

And He *is* seated there perfect, ageless, overflowing with divine health, radiance, magnificence, and all-conquering and all-powerful having risen from the grave conquering death and the forces of darkness forever........*AS HE IS, SO ARE WE IN THIS WORLD*.....BELIEVE IT AND RECEIVE IT....you are more than a conqueror in Christ Jesus!

By utilising our faith in this miracle, we step into our divine higher selves and take on all the characteristics of Jesus Himself.....supernatural strength, power, fortitude, courage, youthfulness, righteousness, radiance, divine health, serenity, joy, temperance, wisdom, compassion, peace, perfect love and heavenly glory!

We aren't called "believers" for nothing. By truly and fully believing in this revelation, you have access to the riches of heaven and a life in which you will be blessed beyond what you can imagine. Jesus was the only pure man who ever walked the earth, pure in body, mind, soul and spirit and with a heart as pure and as white as the driven snow. Believers who receive Jesus take on the heart of Jesus and the righteousness of God. And what is the heart but purity, love and life itself.

PROVERBS 17: 22: "A merry heart doeth good *like* a medicine: but a broken spirit drieth the bones."

Bad thoughts, impure thoughts, evil thoughts, deeds, machinations all originate out of an impure heart, one devoid of righteousness and open to attack by the enemy. The Breastplate of Righteousness must be worn to keep the heart pure and vibrating love, in turn producing loving thoughts, words and actions. And although the breastplate as a piece of armour in the time of the Romans could be taken off after battle, God's foot soldiers do not have that option.

For we are caught in the battle of the ages. It is the war between God and His arch-enemy Satan, and it is ongoing. The earth is the physical battle ground. But the weapons of warfare are not of this world.

2nd CORINTHIANS 10: 4: "(For the weapons of our warfare *are* not carnal, but mighty through God to the pulling down of strong holds;)"

PROVERBS 4: 23 gives the instruction "Keep thy heart with all diligence; for out of it *are* the issues of life".

It is vital we guard our hearts at all times with the Breastplate of Righteousness. The heart is the reflection of the man, his thoughts, his works and his life.

MARK 7: 21: "For from within, out of the heart of men, proceed evil thoughts, adulteries, fornications, murders,"

MARK 7: 22: "Thefts, covetousness, wickedness, deceit, lasciviousness, an evil eye, blasphemy, pride, foolishness:"

MARK 7: 23: "All these evil things come from within, and defile the man."

All these things are the result of an unprotected, exposed and unrighteous heart. Now you might say that the "Righteous" too can commit and do commit these sins and yes it is true. But the Righteous have power in Jesus Christ, power through Grace, power to repent and ask for elevated levels of faith, strength, protection and righteousness.

Righteousness breeds righteous thoughts and righteous living. Righteousness sees the sin as sin and does not deceive itself. Righteousness acknowledges the falling short and knows the sin is forgiven. Righteousness allows us to repent and to seek the face of God once more, not in guilt or shame, but in full confidence as His righteousness.

We are all sinners and will always sin. But righteousness through Grace empowers our walk with God and helps keep our heart protected and filled with unconditional love. The heart is the well-spring of desires. And we want our desires to be worthy of God. Righteousness is thinking, talking, walking and living in the will of God. The Breastplate of Righteousness will help you act uprightly in God's love, and bring you closer to Him. If you do this, see how God will open the windows of heaven upon your life.

NUMBERS 23: 19:   "God *is* not a man, that he should lie; neither the son of man, that he should repent: hath he said, and shall he not do *it*? or hath he spoken, and shall he not make it good?"

3rd JOHN 2:   "Beloved, I wish above all things that

thou mayest prosper and be in health, even as thy soul prospereth."

Put God to the test. His Word is everlasting truth. Think, talk, act in His will. Be robed in righteousness and clothed in Christ Jesus and see if He will not fulfill all of His promises for your health, your prosperity and for your life. Put God to the test…miracles await…

DEUTERONOMY 28: 8: "The lord shall command the blessing upon thee in thy storehouses, and in all that thou settest thine hand unto; and he shall bless thee in the land which the LORD thy god giveth thee."

A blessed life is the fruit of the Righteous. A life blessed in all areas by God. Protect your heart with the Breastplate of Righteousness. Walk upright, strong, steadfast and confident in God's love and protection EVERY DAY.

Jesus is the Lion of the Tribe of Judah. Have the heart of this Lion EVERY DAY. Spread the love in your heart to create ripples of positivity, joy, fun, laughter, peace and harmony towards your family, friends, neighbours and colleagues…a kind word or gesture, a compliment or a smile, a helping hand, being a friend or being a friend in need, simple acts of kindness…let these ripples turn into waves that will wash over the whole world…let these waves become a flood…and may this flood cleanse, purify and bring the global consciousness back into harmony and balance.

4 THE SHOES OF PEACE

EPHESIANS 6: 15:   "And your feet shod with the preparation of the gospel of peace;"

No walk can be relaxed, satisfying, fulfilling or fully enjoyed without your feet enjoying the close company of the right shoes! Least of all our daily walk of life and our walk with God.

As we take to the battlefield of our daily lives, anchored in truth, heart shielded with righteousness, it is time to put on the Shoes of Peace!

The first word Jesus spoke to His disciples after the resurrection was "Peace".

JOHN 20: 19:   "Then the same day at evening, being the first *day* of the week, when the doors were shut where the disciples were assembled for fear of the Jews, came Jesus and stood in the midst, and saith unto them, Peace *be* unto you."

The Hebrew word for peace is "Shalom" and is used as a greeting or indeed as a parting word of farewell. In broader terms this word is rich in blessings expressing wishes of good health, prosperity, tranquility, completeness, wholeness and restfulness and perfect peace.

In PHILIPPIANS 4: 7 we see the promise of shalom peace for all believers: "And the peace of God, which passeth all understanding, shall keep your hearts and minds through Christ Jesus."

As people living in a noisy and chaotic world we are all familiar with those moments of calm and quiet, where we can catch our breath and gently ease into a subtle state of relaxation and appreciation.

A slow stroll in the countryside on a warm summers day, relaxing with a nice book and a soothing cup of your favourite tea, listening to the cheerful sweet song of the birds as you enjoy some gardening, hearing nothing but the divinely powerful sound of the ocean as you take in a breath-taking sunrise…these are moments of "shalom" peace.

Deep down in our subconscious, on a deeper level, somehow we know these moments are not "of this world". They are so much more. They are the physical manifestations of God's promise of a peace which passes all understanding. This promised peace is absolutely essential for the fulfillment of our divine life purpose as born again believers in Jesus Christ.

When we step out our door and into society, the demands on our person, our time, our patience and on the less friendly days, on our sanity are constant and persistent.

Noisy public transport, traffic jams, meetings, appointments, office demands, reports, deadlines, office politics, over-bearing co-workers, texts, tweets, twits, family commitments, shopping, washing, rinsing, drying, bills, birthdays, bad hair days…..the list is endless! A day in the life can really be a struggle and a drain on our emotional and physical resources.

Imagine a 20km hike through rough and rocky terrain….a pair of shoddy old slippers is going to make for miles of misery! But equipped with the right shoes you'll march purposefully, steadily, comfortably, safely and securely towards your destination. The right footwear facilitates a peaceful and comfortable journey.

Shod in the Shoes of Peace, we have laid the foundation for a successful daily walk and a richly rewarding walk with God.

If there is no peace in our hearts then there can be no peace in our lives. The Gospel of Jesus Christ *is* the Gospel of Peace and believers walking in Him will walk daily in shalom peace, wholeness, restfulness and completeness.

No matter the weather, no matter the season, no matter the circumstance or situation, a believer's walk with God through Jesus Christ, is filled with a peace that surpasses all understanding. It doesn't matter what is happening around you, because you live from the inside out and not the outside in. And inside you is Jesus Christ and working through you is the Holy Spirit.

Assaults on the flesh and the senses are met by responses in the Spirit, utilising all of the wonderfully rich and supernaturally powerful blessings we receive as believers in Christ...for "...greater is he that is in you, than he that is in the world." - 1st JOHN 4: 4

In chapter 2, verse 20 of St. Paul's Epistle to the GALATIANS, we see the power made available to us to meet and masterfully overcome all of the trials and tribulations of daily living:

"I am crucified with Christ: nevertheless I live; yet not I, but Christ liveth in me: and the life which I now live in the flesh I live by the faith of the Son of God, who loved me, and gave himself for me."

As a born-again believer, it is no longer you who lives but Jesus who lives in you. Jesus Christ whilst being fully man was also fully God, in the form of man…..and if God be for you, who can be against you?

Be in the world, but not of it. Be not in the values of the world, rather "…seek ye first the kingdom of God, and his righteousness; and all these things shall be added unto you." – MATTHEW 6: 33

…for in God's economy, the meek shall inherit the earth and a lamb sits upon the throne.

Jesus said…

"Peace I leave with you, my peace I give unto you: not as the world giveth, give I unto you. Let not your heart be troubled, neither let it be afraid." - JOHN 14: 27:

Step away from the world and into Jesus, EVERY DAY of your life and walk successfully, safely, comfortably and securely in a Peace which passes all understanding.

5 THE SHIELD OF FAITH

EPHESIANS 6: 16: "Above all, taking the shield of faith, wherewith ye shall be able to quench all the fiery darts of the wicked."

Grounded in the truth and the Word of God, standing tall and strong in the Breastplate of Righteousness and walking safe and securely in the Shoes of Peace, it is time for the Divine Soldier to take up the Shield…

…without an impenetrable shield, any soldier is wide open to direct attack on any and every part of the body. He is a sitting duck. For the Soldier of God, the Bible states "Above all, taking the shield…". Scripture stresses the importance of the Shield of Faith. As believers we are nothing without faith. Faith is the foundation of our very lives, the rock upon which our spiritual house is built.

MATTHEW 7: 24: "Therefore whosoever heareth these sayings of mine, and doeth them, I will liken him to a wise man, which built his house upon a rock:"

MATTHEW 7: 25: "And the rain descended, and the floods came, and the winds blew, and beat upon that house; and it fell not: for it was founded upon a rock."

Without faith a believer is not a believer. Without faith we cannot receive Jesus as Lord and Saviour. Without faith we do not have the Holy Spirit working through us and for us. Without faith we do not truly believe in God. Without faith we are not spiritual warriors marching victoriously in full Divine Armour, we are hapless and helpless souls wandering aimlessly a fierce battleground, unarmed, unprotected and exposed to every fiery dart of the enemy.

The modus operandi of any enemy is to attack and to inflict pain, suffering and death either figuratively or literally. The arch-enemy of God attacks constantly and persistently and with a supernatural intensity.

The Bible says in JOHN 10: 10 "The thief cometh not, but for to steal, and to kill, and to destroy…" The verse goes on "…I am come that they might have life, and that they might have *it* more abundantly."

The devil has come to attack and bring death and destruction. Jesus has come to bring life, and life more abundantly. The battlefield is our awe-inspiringly beautiful planet earth and our very lives.

Jesus Christ is our shield. Through our faith in Him we must raise the shield up to rebuke every attack of the enemy. Without our Shield of Faith, without Jesus, we are exposed to attack by one of the fallen Archangels of God, Lucifer himself. Without our Shield of Faith we are unarmed walking flesh, open to assault by a supernatural adversary with supernatural weapons. And this enemy is bitter, twisted, resentful, enraged and filled with an intense hatred for God's creation.

Jesus Christ is our General. He is our rock, our shield and our carnal and spiritual refuge. He is the conqueror of death and the devil through His death on the Cross and resurrection and ascension into heaven where He takes his rightful place at the Father's right hand. And through Him we are "more than conquerors" – ROMANS 8: 37

Through His precious blood we are redeemed, saved, forgiven and forever protected.

ISAIAH 53: 5: "But he *was* wounded for our

transgressions, *he was* bruised for our iniquities: the chastisement of our peace *was* upon him; and with his stripes we are healed."

The Bible states in black and white that Jesus was "wounded for our transgressions...bruised for our iniquities"

...If the Son of Man Himself was wounded in the battle of the ages, and was put to death in our natural world, having given himself up freely, then without Him as our shield, how much more are *we* open to being wounded, mere mortals as we are? Jesus became our sin and received death.

ROMANS 6: 23: "For the wages of sin *is* death; but the gift of God *is* eternal life through Jesus Christ our Lord."

Thank God for His ultimate act of love, the sacrificing of His only begotten Son for our salvation and everlasting life through Him.

The Bible calls the devil "the accuser of our brethren".

REVELATION 12: 10: "And I heard a loud voice saying in heaven, Now is come salvation, and strength, and the kingdom of our God, and the power of his Christ: for the accuser of our brethren is cast down, which accused them before our God day and night."

The devil will constantly accuse you. He will whisper subtle accusations that you are no good or not good enough, that you're not worthy, you're not smart enough, you're not rich enough, you're not pretty enough, you're emotionally weak, he will constantly remind you of your faults and past failings, planting seeds of doubt suggesting it didn't work then, what makes you think it will work now? He will plant seeds of fear to keep you in bondage and hold you back from your true self which is as a child of the most High God, a divine being living in the natural world.

It is written in 1st PETER 5: 8:   "Be sober, be vigilant; because your adversary the devil, as a roaring lion, walketh about, seeking whom he may devour:"

His accusations will be most intense at times when we are close to breakthrough or when we are at our most tired. Be sober, be vigilant and extra so at these times. All of the weapons of the enemy, sin, fear, deception, guilt, shame, condemnation, sickness, poverty, negativity, bitterness, resentment, worry, doubt, anxiety, misdirected and uncontrolled anger, depression, prolonged sorrow or grief, pride, greed, lust, laziness, self-pity, low self-esteem, distraction, procrastination, jealousy, envy were all destroyed at the Cross.

God will never whisper an accusation. Every voice like this that you hear, it is not yours. They are not your thoughts. It is the accusations of the accuser of the brethren. So pay them no heed. Take no notice of them. Pay them no attention. Recognise and acknowledge them for what they are, then continue on your victorious walk with God.

As believers, our faith in Jesus has made us the righteousness of God. And our Shield of Faith forever protects us from those fiery darts of the enemy.

So lift up the shield, raise it high EVERY DAY of your life, and march on more than a conqueror in total victory.

6 THE HELMET OF SALVATION

EPHESIANS 6: 17:   "And take the helmet of salvation, and the sword of the spirit, which is the word of God:"

With the Shield of Faith raised high, our battle march requires the final piece of protective armour.

A sense of awareness, a keen eye, good hearing and a sharp and clear mind are key attributes for any soldier. For the divine foot-soldier, the Helmet of Salvation is of paramount importance in guarding our eyes, ears, our brain and so our mind.

2nd TIMOTHY 1: 7:   "For God hath not given us the spirit of fear; but of power, and of love, and of a sound mind."

Fear is not a natural state of mind and does not come from God. Fear is learned. And anything learned can be unlearned. God is love and through His Son Jesus we are love. It is the essence of our being, our divine and natural state. Perfect and unconditional love.

1st JOHN 4: 18:   "There is no fear in love; but perfect love casteth out fear: because fear hath torment. He that feareth is not made perfect in love."

1st JOHN 4: 20:   "If a man say, I love God, and hateth his brother, he is a liar: for he that loveth not his brother whom he hath seen, how can he love God whom he hath not seen?"

…Hear this word of God.

1st CORINTHIANS 2: 12 states "Now we have received, not the spirit of the world, but the spirit which is of God…"

1st CORINTHIANS 2: 16 declares: "For who hath known the mind of the Lord, that he may instruct him? But we have the mind of Christ."

As believers, we have the mind of Christ. Through Calvary, the blood and death of Jesus on the Cross, salvation was and is offered to all. For believers who are in Jesus, putting on the Helmet of Salvation gives us the mind of Christ. This is the Word of God. And it is the same yesterday, today and forever.

For many this truth will be a mind-blowing concept and quite a revelation. This incredible gift allows believers to fully live in, work in and operate in our physical natural world but with a supernatural power and mind-set.

There flows a wisdom that is not of this world to deal more than effectively with the challenges of daily living. There is not the rigid and fixed attachment to the world that so many people try to live under, rather an ease of spirit, a deep and peaceful knowing of the things of this world for what they are and their relative importance or lack thereof.

There is not the constant, manic, must be moving, must be doing, must be fixing, must be solving, must, must, "have to" mentality that drains the body and mind of poise, energy and peace. Rather there is a quiet and calm acceptance of things as they are and the knowledge that everything is in divine order and exactly as it should be at that moment in time.

For believers in Christ with the mind of Christ, have a deep-rooted and unwavering belief in themselves through Jesus, and an unshakeable faith in God and His good intentions for their lives.

JEREMIAH 29: 11: "For I know the thoughts that I think toward you, saith the LORD, thoughts of peace, and not of evil, to give you an expected end."

ROMANS 8: 28: "And we know that all things work together for good to them that love God, to them who are called according to *his* purpose."

...this is the knowledge that allows believers to stay firmly anchored in Christ Jesus and the Word of God, no matter the circumstance or situation, the trial or the tribulation happening in the world around them.

The mind of Christ is a tranquil, peaceful and serene getaway from an all too frequently clamorous, contentious and chaotic world....more simply put, the mind of Christ allows us to be in the world but not of it.

2nd TIMOTHY 2: 4: "No man that warreth entangleth himself with the affairs of *this* life; that he may please him who hath chosen him to be a soldier."

The Helmet of Salvation is essential for total victory in the battlefield of our mind and in our daily lives.

It is the watchman that stands guard at the door of our mind. It helps keep our thoughts pure and in alignment with the will and the Word of God.

It is our mental and moral compass, firmly fixing the needle on our true north which is the will, the Word and the workings of God.

It is the peace of God which passes all understanding, keeping our hearts and our minds through Jesus

Christ.

It is the protective visor, the spiritual lens that helps focus and re-focus the carnal eye for "...whosoever looketh on a woman to lust after her hath committed adultery with her already in his heart." – MATTHEW 5: 28

It is the helmet that helps keep our ears attuned to our higher-selves, for "...faith *cometh* by hearing, and hearing by the word of God" - ROMANS 10: 17

It is our supernatural sensor, readily detecting and destroying any incoming attack on our godliness and our godly mission "Casting down imaginations, and every high thing that exalteth itself against the knowledge of God, and bringing into captivity every thought to the obedience of Christ;" - 2nd CORINTHIANS 10: 5

It is our protective filter against toxic thoughts, for "...whatsoever things are true, whatsoever things *are* honest, whatsoever things *are* just, whatsoever things *are* pure, whatsoever things *are* lovely, whatsoever things *are* of good report; if *there be* any virtue, and if *there be* any praise, think on these things." – PHILIPPIANS 4: 8

The enemy is the accuser of the brethren and wars day and night against believers and non-believers alike trying to infiltrate the stronghold of their mind. But only a believer has the defences strong enough to resist his fiery attacks. For believers possess the mind of Christ. They know that the victory has already been won. It was won at Calvary on the Cross through the blood of Jesus. And that victory is eternal.

This fundamental and absolute knowing of being under siege in a battle that has already been won, allows believers to thwart any attack through faith alone.

The weapons of the enemy, from sickness to poverty, negativity to fear, doubt, anxiety and depression, were all destroyed at the Cross…and the mind of Christ knows this full well. For believers are assured through the living Word that "No weapon that is formed against thee shall prosper…" – ISAIAH 54: 17

The miracle of salvation through the death and resurrection of Jesus, allows believers to rest, find hope, have optimism and experience peace, even in the most difficult and demanding circumstances that we all, as people living in a fallen world, inevitably experience.

MATTHEW 11: 28: "Come unto me, all *ye* that labour and are heavy laden, and I will give you rest."

JOHN 16: 33: "These things I have spoken unto you, that in me ye might have peace. In the world ye shall have tribulation: but be of good cheer; I have overcome the world."

The Helmet of Salvation gives us the mind of Christ and helps keep our mind on Christ. By putting on the helmet EVERY DAY, our mind will be transformed. And like exercise building muscle, this habitual action will strengthen our mind daily, bringing our thoughts more and more in alignment with the Word of God and His divine purpose for our lives.

Like the mightiest portcullis that protects the castle, our mind will be shut to negative influences and attacks from all enemies, and instead be open to a constant and flowing stream of Godly wisdom, love and compassion. This stream will gather momentum as it gathers strength and will become a gushing river, effortlessly carrying forth otherworldly levels of joy, hope, optimism and belief in the potential in ourselves, in people, and in the world.

PSALMS 82: 6: "I have said, Ye *are* Gods; and all of you *are* children of the most High."

It is time to ask yourself what you believe. Look around you. What do you see? How do you feel? Do you believe the things that men have told you that you are?

PSALMS 118: 8: "*It is* better to trust in the LORD than to put confidence in man."

The Lord God of heaven and earth through His living Word has told you "…Ye *are* Gods; and all of you *are* children of the most High."

What does any son or daughter carry in them?

…The DNA of their Father…

…Whether you are a believer or non-believer, throughout your body is intricately, inextricably and miraculously woven the supernatural DNA of the Creator of the heavens and the earth.

Salvation is yours and thereby freedom from any and all bondage to anything that is not of God. Pick up the Helmet EVERY DAY. Put it on. Your armour is complete. You are ready for battle. You are more than equipped. You are more than a conqueror in Christ Jesus.

Step away from the troubles of the world. Be triumphant. The victory has already been won. Revel in this knowledge. Let it catapult you forward to places and things in this life that you never dreamed you could see. March forward in full confidence and full of joy. For it is time to fully enjoy living again. Everything has been taken care of. Rest and feel at peace. Your salvation has been guaranteed…

…Rise up…

…YE…ARE…GODS!

7 THE SWORD OF THE SPIRIT

EPHESIANS 6: 17: "And take the helmet of salvation, and the sword of the Spirit, which is the word of God."

JOHN 1: 1: "In the beginning was the Word, and the Word was with God, and the Word was God."

With the Helmet of Salvation securely fastened, your Divine Armour is complete. All of your vital bodily and spiritual organs are now under supernatural protection. Defensively you are rock-solid. But no soldier is fully prepared without a good weapon at his side to go on the offensive. The Divine Soldier of God possesses the greatest weapon ever known – The Sword of the Spirit.

After 40 days and nights of fasting in the wilderness, the devil came to Jesus, like a roaring lion looking to devour him. Knowing His obvious hunger and state of weariness he began to tempt him:

MATTHEW 4: 3: "And when the tempter came to him, he said, If thou be the Son of God, command that these stones be made bread."

Jesus answered, "…It is written, Man shall not live by bread alone, but by every word that proceedeth out of the mouth of God." - MATTHEW 4: 4

Under attack by the greatest adversary of the Creator of the heavens and the earth, Jesus responded by saying "…IT…IS…WRITTEN…"

The greatest weapon you can ever possess is the written Word of God.

The Divine Soldier's weapon *is* the Word of God. And it is the most powerful weapon in all of creation.

HEBREWS 4: 12: "For the word of God *is* quick, and powerful, and sharper than any twoedged sword, piercing even to the dividing asunder of soul and spirit, and of the joints and marrow, and *is* a discerner of the thoughts and intents of the heart."

Twice more the devil tried Jesus:

MATTHEW 4: 6: "…If thou be the Son of God, cast thyself down: for it is written, He shall give his angels charge concerning thee: and in *their* hands they shall bear thee up, lest at any time thou dash thy foot against a stone."

Jesus replied, "…It is written again, Thou shalt not tempt the Lord thy God." – MATTHEW 4: 7

The devil tried him a third time: "Again, the devil taketh him up into an exceeding high mountain, and sheweth him all the kingdoms of the world, and the glory of them; And saith unto him, All these things will I give thee, if thou wilt fall down and worship me." – MATTHEW 4: 8-9

Again Jesus rebuked him: "…Get thee hence, Satan: for it is written, Thou shalt worship the Lord thy God, and him only shalt thou serve." – MATTHEW 4: 10

As believers we are to follow the example of Jesus, His ways, His works and His words. There is no more critical or pressing example to follow than His rebuke of the devil in the wilderness by the Sword of the Spirit.

PROVERBS 18: 21: "Death and life *are* in the power of the tongue: and they that love it shall eat the fruit thereof."

We have been given the example and the power to speak life to any situation and to cut down quickly and decisively any attack on our body, mind, soul or spirit.

Speak to the problem. Speak to the attack. Speak to the negative voice trying to poison your mind. Speak to the sickness. Speak to the devour, lack or poverty. Speak to that area of famine or despair in your life, for death and life *are* in the power of the tongue. This *is* the Word of God.

JOHN 1: 1:   "In the beginning was the Word, and the Word was with God, and the Word was God."

God was then and is now…the Word was God… and the Word remains God and as God is living, so too is His Word living. The Bible is the living Word of God. And therein, it is a book of supernatural power.

When you find yourself under attack by that negative seed trying to take root in your mind, your body or your life, speak to it, speak out loud…

…say the words, believe them, "Let not your heart be troubled…" - JOHN 14: 1, or "No weapon that is formed against thee shall prosper…" - ISAIAH 54: 17….say it in your mind, then say it out loud….change the "thee" to "me"…"NO WEAPON FORMED   AGAINST   ME   SHALL PROSPER"….the attack is not easily averted, most often there will come the second wave….rebuke it, repeat the words, speak to that accusation, that attack …"IT……IS…….WRITTEN……NO   WEAPON

FORMED AGAINST ME SHALL PROSPER…..LET NOT YOUR HEART BE TROUBLED"…..

….step back a moment and see…..you are now standing steadfast and strong in full Divine Armour, wielding the Sword of the Spirit in a death blow to that attack.

God the Father, whose love for us is beyond our grasp of understanding has provided everything we need for total protection and total prosperity in our lives. This provision is His living Word. And it is a miracle.

The Bible contains many verses concerning all of the problems we as people living in a fallen world may face.

ON PHYSICAL HEALING

As is often said "your health is your wealth". And never a truer word. The Bible contains a multitude of verses that contain the power to physically heal.

One of the names of God in the Bible is "Jehovah Rapha" or "Our God who heals"

In EXODUS 15: 26 it is written, "...for I *am* the Lord that healeth thee."

Our God is Jehovah Rapha, the Great Physician.

1st JOHN 5: 4: "For whatsoever is born of God overcometh the world: and this is the victory that overcometh the world, *even* our faith."

The Word of God clearly declares God's wish for us to be in good health and to prosper:

3rd JOHN 2: "Beloved, I wish above all things that thou mayest prosper and be in health, even as thy soul prospereth."

The Gospel of Matthew describes the story of the woman with the issue of blood who had been afflicted 12 years. When the woman heard that Jesus was coming to town she said, "…If I may but touch his garment, I shall be whole." – MATTHEW 9: 21

After succeeding in touching his garment, Jesus' response was, "…Daughter, be of good comfort; thy faith hath made thee whole…" – MATTHEW 9: 22

The connection here between faith and healing is unequivocal and undeniable. Whilst we no longer have the opportunity to go out and physically touch the garment of Jesus, we have been touched by Jesus Himself.

GALATIANS 2: 20:   "I am crucified with Christ: nevertheless I live; yet not I, but Christ liveth in me: and the life which I now live in the flesh I live by the faith of the Son of God, who loved me, and gave himself for me."

PSALMS 103: 2-3:   "Bless the Lord, O my soul, and forget not all his benefits: Who forgiveth all thine iniquities; who healeth all thy diseases;"

ISAIAH 53: 5:   "…with his stripes we are healed."

As we can see, the bible is alive with the written Word expressly declaring its power to heal. Jesus, as well as bearing all of our sins on the Cross, also bore all of our sicknesses and diseases, destroyed forever so that we might have life and have it more abundantly.

But just as with the woman with the issue of blood, who had absolute faith in the power to be healed, our faith in God's promise, in His Word, in His provision and in the accomplished work of the Cross at Calvary is essential to activate the miracle blessings and healing power of Jehovah Rapha, our God who heals.

We are blessed with the wisdom and expertise of doctors in the medical profession and the advancements in this field. They are an essential part of treating health issues, sickness and disease.

Should the situation ever arise where we need specialist help for a serious illness, we would never bypass the foremost treatment, or the leading authorities on the area in question. Why is it then, even as believers, that we dismiss out of hand the potential healing power of the living Word?

It is written that "My people are destroyed for lack of knowledge…" – HOSEA 4: 6

Our Lord who heals is the Creator of all things. He is the greatest physician in heaven and on earth. He is the leading authority in all things. And should always have the final say or verdict on areas related to health, as in all things.

NUMBERS 23: 19:   "God *is* not a man, that he should lie…"

3rd JOHN 2:   "Beloved, I wish above all things that thou mayest prosper and be in health, even as thy soul prospereth."

As God is the Great Physician, so we are the patient. Our co-operation, our faith, is the prescription God has handed down to us. And our medicine is His living Word, given to cure our sickness, to heal our bodies and to be made whole.

God is also sovereign and we cannot begin to understand the infinite depths of Him or how He works in the world. However we do have His Word, and it is infallible truth. And it is where we should place our trust, our hope and our faith.

If the medical report gives no hope, then what hope left is there? The answer is the *Great* hope. Jehovah Rapha. God our healer.

It is your body, your life. Or the life of a loved one or friend maybe. It is time to ask yourself what you believe.

God does not respond to circumstance, or to tears not born of faith. He only responds to faith and faith-based prayer. Take Him at his Word, for His Word is living and brings life. Speak to that sickness in your body, rebuke it, cut through it with the Sword of the

Spirit…"In the name of Jesus, I take authority over any spirit of sickness in my body, and command it to leave NOW".

The Bible says in JOHN 14: 14: "If ye shall ask any thing in my name, I will do *it*."

Be specific. When rebuking the sickness, name the sickness. Be it depression, anxiety, diabetes, high blood pressure, cancer, heart-disease, insomnia, whatever it is, in the name of Jesus, claim authority over that unclean spirit attacking your body.

Name the sickness and speak the words, "…I take authority over you in the name of Jesus, I rebuke you, I command you to leave this body NOW in Jesus' name."

In the natural, this concept can be difficult to grasp…but this is precisely the point. We are not dealing purely with the natural, we are introducing supernatural power to the natural, to deal a death blow to foreign bodies trying to attack and poison *our* bodies. And we are connecting to this supernatural life-line by means of our faith.

…"…these signs shall follow them that believe; In my name shall they cast out devils; they shall speak with new tongues; They shall take up serpents; and if they drink any deadly thing, it shall not hurt them; they shall lay hands on the sick, and they shall recover." - MARK 16: 17-18

As in the time of the Romans, when the soldier could find himself isolated and behind enemy lines, with help far off...the Sword can be the weapon that will save your life.

Leave the timetable of recovery and healing up to God. But wield the Sword of the Spirit daily in absolute faith.

"For verily I say unto you, That whosoever shall say unto this mountain, Be thou removed, and be thou cast into the sea; and shall not doubt in his heart, but shall believe that those things which he saith shall come to pass; he shall have whatsoever he saith." - MARK 11: 23

Speak life to that sickness and trust God to heal.

ON EMOTIONAL HEALING

2nd CORINTHIANS 12: 9: "And he said unto me, My grace is sufficient for thee: for my strength is made perfect in weakness. Most gladly therefore will I rather glory in my infirmities, that the power of Christ may rest upon me."

2nd CORINTHIANS 12: 10: "Therefore I take pleasure in infirmities, in reproaches, in necessities, in persecutions, in distresses for Christ's sake: for when I am weak, then am I strong."

As well as the power for physical healing, the Scripture contains divine wisdom with the power for emotional healing.

PSALMS 34: 15: "The eyes of the LORD *are* upon the righteous, and his ears *are open* unto their cry."

Be it the loss of a job, the break-up of a relationship or a marriage, the loss of a loved-one or indeed any emotional distress, the Lord has assured us that He will hear our cry, comfort us and help us to heal.

PSALMS 147: 3: "He healeth the broken in heart, and bindeth up their wounds."

...a comforting thought to say the least.

The Lord has assured us that during the most testing of circumstances and in our darkest hour, He *will* be there. He will comfort us and give us strength, for His strength "is made perfect in weakness."

Remember the Lord in times of distress, seek His comfort, draw near to Him and He has promised he will draw near to you.

PSALMS 145: 18: "The LORD *is* nigh unto all them that call upon him, to all that call upon him in truth."

Trust in the Lord. Your heart will be healed. Hear His Word and rest in His loving and comforting embrace.

ON FINANCIAL PROSPERITY

One of the names of God in the Bible is Jehovah Jira, "the Lord our provider".

The Word of the Lord makes it clear that His wish for us is that we may prosper in all things; this includes financial prosperity.

DEUTERONOMY 8: 18: "But thou shalt remember the LORD thy God: for *it is* he that giveth thee power to get wealth…"

Poverty and lack are not of God. In times such as these, seek counsel from the Holy Spirit, for God has assured us of His blessing.

PROVERBS 10: 22: "The blessing of the Lord, it maketh rich, and he added no sorrow with it."

PSALMS 34: 10: "The young lions do lack, and suffer hunger: but they that seek the LORD shall not want any good *thing*."

The law of sowing and reaping is a universal law.

The Bible says in GALATIANS 6: 8: "For he that soweth to his flesh shall of the flesh reap corruption; but he that soweth to the Spirit shall of the Spirit reap life everlasting."

…the flesh brings corruption…the Spirit brings life.

This universal law of sowing and reaping works perfectly throughout every aspect of life.

Just as the sowing of a little acorn will in time produce a mighty oak, the sowing of a financial seed will produce a financial harvest.

MALACHI 3: 10: "Bring ye all the tithes into the storehouse, that there may be meat in mine house, and prove me now herewith, saith the LORD of hosts, if I will not open you the windows of heaven, and pour you out a blessing, that *there shall* not *be room* enough *to receive* it."

The importance of tithing in the Bible, to produce wealth, cannot be underestimated.

PROVERBS 3: 9-10: "Honour the LORD with thy substance, and with the firstfruits of all thine increase: So shall thy barns be filled with plenty, and thy presses shall burst out with new wine."

The Bible says Abraham tithed "…a tenth part of all…" – HEBREWS 7: 2

God is not moved by circumstance or situation, He is only moved by faith.

Through His Word, God is telling us, if you have faith in Me, in My Word, then your financial seed sown in the earth shall reap a harvest rained down from heaven.

It's interesting how many non-believers and believers alike will put their faith and their lives in the hands of an airline pilot whom they have never seen or met, and they will trust the banks with their money, but they will not trust God.

Give generously to your church. Give to a ministry that you feel connected with. Give to a good cause or a worthwhile project. Give to the poor. Give with a pure heart and with confident expectation through your faith in God's Word and "...it shall be given unto you; good measure, pressed down, and shaken together, and running over...For with the same measure that ye mete withal it shall be measured to you again." – LUKE 6: 38

Speak to that area of lack in your life. Speak life into that time of financial famine. Speak your confidence in God's truth and in His Word. And sow a financial seed in confident expectation of a supernatural harvest that will change your life.

Through the Sword of the Spirit you have been given the power to speak life back into any area of your life that is under attack, be it your health, your family, your marriage, your relationships, your job, your finances, even your faith.

Remember your divine power in Jesus Christ through the Divine Armour of God and through the supernatural power of the Sword of the Spirit, which is God's holy and everlasting truth. He *is* the Creator of all things. And He has given us the power through His beloved Son, to wield His Word as an all-powerful weapon that will cut through every attack from this world and beyond.

8 THE DIVINE SOLDIER

When Jesus was nailed to the Cross at Calvary, His Divine Armour fell to the ground. The weapon of His condemners pierced His side, spilling His blood, whereby the ground, the armour, the whole world was instantly washed clean and purified, as He cried out "It is finished".

Jesus, in this moment, passed His mantle to us. His work was finished, complete. He died for all, so that all might be forever cleansed of all sins and spared the judgement of sinners.

The punishment we deserved as sinners, He bore with every excrutiating blood-soaked stripe and with every nail mercilessly hammered into flesh and bone. In return we received unmerited favour, amazing Grace and salvation. The only caveat, the only condition....that we believe through faith that He died for these reasons, that we repent of our sins and that we make Him the Lord of our lives.

Live joyfully EVERY DAY in this knowledge. Stand tall, upright and strong to honour His incredible sacrifice and so that the unimaginable pain suffered by the only pure and innocent man who ever lived, is not in vain.

When we live in fear, guilt, shame, in condemnation, with anxiety, worry, poor self-image or lack of hope, we are rejecting Jesus and the sacrifice He made for us. We are rejecting God and His ultimate sacrifice.

Fear, depression, anxiety, negativity, bitterness, doubt, unforgiveness are all of the enemy, and a daily lifestyle of living under these low-vibrational clouds, is a life of bondage to God's enemy. You are his. You are in chains, living the illusion of freedom. Powerless. Lost. But not without hope.

Be brave. Have courage. Have heart. Be of good cheer. Jesus Christ is the way, the truth and the life. And His divine offer that he made 2,000 years ago at Calvary still stands today. Deliverance, freedom, salvation are yours. Invite Him in. He will come. Your life will never be the same.

Jesus will raise you up as a high-flying standard sparkling in the morning sun. He will be the friend that will never, ever leave you. He will be with you always. It *is* His promise, "...*even* unto the end of the world". – MATTHEW 28: 20

His Holy Spirit will forever be your supernatural mentor, counsellor and guide. And "…the fruit of the Spirit is love, joy, peace, longsuffering, gentleness, goodness, faith, Meekness, temperance: against such there is no law." – GALATIANS 5: 22-23.

Jesus said, "Verily, verily, I say unto you, He that believeth on me, the works that I do shall he do also; and greater *works* than these shall he do; because I go unto my Father." - JOHN 14: 12

…and "…these signs shall follow them that believe; In my name shall they cast out devils; they shall speak with new tongues; They shall take up serpents; and if they drink any deadly thing, it shall not hurt them; they shall lay hands on the sick, and they shall recover." - MARK 16: 17-18

It is time. Stand up. Be counted. Take up your mantle. Step into the Divine Armour. It is a perfect fit for a child of God. Raise the Sword and the Shield. Stand ready, in complete protection and total victory. You *are* a Divine Soldier of God. And you are not alone. All around you are like-minded warriors. Seek them out. Come together. And if they do not already know, tell them about the Divine Armour. Your General will be most pleased…

…through the Divine Armour of God, you will be

strengthened and protected EVERY DAY, in EVERY area of your life, through the life-giving fruit and the holy blessings of God's living Word...

...and your house shall forever be built upon a rock. Unshakeable. Immovable. Eternal.

THE AARONIC BLESSING – given by God Himself to Moses:

"The LORD bless thee, and keep thee:

The LORD make his face shine upon thee,

And be gracious unto thee:

The LORD lift up his countenance upon thee,

And give thee peace."

...Finally, DIVINE SOLDIER OF GOD...Hear now the Word of your General...

"Be strong and of a good courage; be not afraid, neither be thou dismayed: for the LORD thy God *is* with thee whithersoever thou goest."

"*El Shaddai*…"…the troubled voice cried out again…

…finally, after what seemed like an age but was only an instant…

…a loud voice was heard, clear and pure as the morning dew, ringing true like the golden blasts of the trumpets of victory…

"*ARISE* soldier…..take up the Armour, raise the Shield and wield the Sword….you are ready….

…YE…ARE…GODS"

- General "El Shaddai" - "God Almighty" -

THE END

ABOUT THE AUTHOR

Ramsey Watchman is a 40 year old follower of our Lord and Saviour Jesus Christ. He is a musician and writer and lives in Dublin Ireland.

Printed in Great Britain
by Amazon

74917922R00050